A COMPLETE GUIDE TO RAW FEEDING YOUR CATS AND DOGS

Content

Introduction

Nicole is a certified Pet Nutritionist who has studied extensively   how to identify the best possible balanced diet each individual dog or cat needs. She is able to recommend ways of how to prevent certain health problems occurring such as parasites and diseases, and help identify common conditions, viruses and bugs that your pet may suffer from and how to fight them.

In this book Nicole shares her knowledge, experience and recommendations about feeding a well balanced raw diet.

*After reading the book and transitioning to either raw, it is always recommended to consult with your **holistic vet** or **pet nutritionist**.*

There are a lot of conflicting theories and myths about what to feed our dogs and cats. This can get very confusing about what the best approach is to ensure a healthy long life style for our pets, especially when these myths are coming from people to earn a profit or lack knowledge about pet nutrition. This book will help clarify a lot of questions some people may have about raw feeding and put the myths to rest. It may be a lot of information to take in all at once, however I do assure you that it is not as complicated as it seems.

This book is for
   -People interested to transition their dog or cat to a a raw diet
   -People who already raw feed and want to ensure that they are feeding the right quantities, variation and balance
   -Learn the benefits of raw feeding
   -Different types of raw feeding
   -Wether or not to supplement the dog or cat
   -Recipe ideas for DIY

Poor nutrition in dogs and cats reflects not only the insides but also the exterior. A poor diet means having a low immune system, resulting in a number of issues such as skeletal problems, joint health and bone

Benefits of Fresh Feeding

- Their skin and coat changes drastically to the better once fed raw. It becomes silky and shiny. This is because of the fats and oils that are fed naturally.
- Raw meaty bones help with oral and dental hygiene, giving their jaw a good work out and keeps them mentally stimulated. Chewing releases endorphins which in turn relaxes the dog or cat and reduces anxiety. It removes tartar on the teeth and avoids unnecessary bacteria to build up
- Fresh is always better as no additives are added to the food. It improves "sensitive" stomachs. As raw food is not processed or cooked all the nutrients are stored and not wasted. Faeces are therefore smaller and less frequent because the body is absorbing all nutrients and not releasing fillers and additives that they do not need.
- Raw feeding can be adjusted to your pet's needs depending on his or her medical history, life stage and behaviour.

Anatomy of A Dog

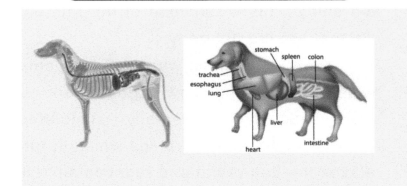

Anatomy of a Cat

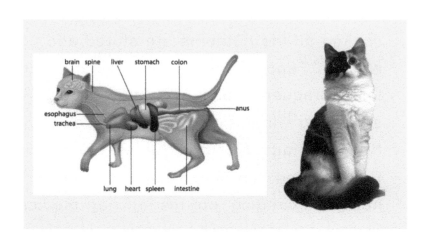

Anatomy of a dog is designed differently to ours, starting with their mouth, teeth and jaw. They are designed to tear down meat and the molars are solely designed to crunch bones. Their bite has enough pressure to devour large parts of an animal. Their mouth and throat is able to open wide enough to swallow huge pieces and leave the stomach to digest.

A dog's gut is around four times their body length as opposed to a human gut that is ten to eleven times your body. The short gut and low PH makes them a perfect example of why dogs are made to eat meat, making food move very fast in the gut and giving no time for bacteria to colonise. Having a low PH means containing a high acidic level. As they are eating meat, the dog's stomach grinds and releases acid, something which their stomach does not do when eating dry food. As the digestive system is not operating as it should be when on dry food, the PH level rises to one that is not healthy or recommended.

Dogs are very resilient to bacteria. Their saliva contains an enzyme called lysozyme, which destroys harmful bacteria.

Cats are true carnivores with a short digestive tract. Carnivores eat a meat/whole prey diet only.

Cats same as dogs that are fed a balanced raw diet or a home cooked meal have a higher acidic stomach then those fed biscuits, dry food and wet food. Cats also have antibacterial salivary enzymes together with a short gut. When raw fed or home cooked they are less likely to develop illness from exposure to pathogens.

For cats, taurine is necessary for brain, nerves, eyes, heart, digestion, immune function and fetal development. For dogs, taurine is needed for eyes, reproduction, bile acid (for fat digestion) and for healthy heart.

Cats require more taurine in their diet than dogs. The daily taurine dietary requirements for a cat is 320mg/kg of food per day. During gestation and lactation cats require 450mg of taurine per day. Chicken hearts are a great source of taurine.

Notes

Basic Differences Feeding
Dogs and Cats

Dogs and cats have different dietary requirements. Cats are true carnivores, whilst dogs are known to be facultative omnivores, some may call them facultative carnivores. The difference is that dogs regularly eat a variety of material including plants, animals, algae and fungi. They require a lower protein diet than cats. Cats thrive on a high protein diet. Some people may debate the fact wether dogs are actually facultative omnivores or carnivores. By definition facultative omnivores means that they are not obligate carnivores but need meat as their main source of protein. Dogs can live on meat, bones and organs alone or have vegetables and fruits added to their diet. Cats thrive solely on meat, bone and organs.

Cats cannot fast for more than 24 hours otherwise they can suffer from hepatic lipidosis. Cats are much bigger fussy eaters than dogs, therefore it is always recommended to transition the cat slowly if he or she does not take into raw food immediately. Although it is not advised to mix commercial food with raw, in this case it would benefit the cat more to transition him or her slowly. Cats need to eat something everyday. They require a diet that includes amino acid arginine and taurine, as cats do not produce these amino acids like dogs. Taurine is an essential nutrient found in all meats, especially hearts.

Safe Bones to Feed

> **BONES SHOULD ALWAYS BE FED RAW AND NEVER COOKED.**
> Never leave a dog or a cat unsupervised whilst eating.

Safe bones

Bones that are safe to feed, chew and digest are light weight bones such as chicken, turkey, quail, duck, pheasant and rabbit. Any other bones should be properly minced.

Recreational bones

These are weight bearing bones which are only given as a treat and not edible. They are not bones which can be swallowed, however they are given to dogs to strip off meat while working their jaws and clean their teeth. Once meat has been stripped of, the bone must be removed to avoid teeth getting fractured or bone swallowed.

Example or recreational bones are bone marrow and beef knuckle bones. When feeding recreational bone like bone marrow make su that they are halved like th pic. This avoids the bone getting stuck in the mouth causing injuries.

Chicken Feet

- rich in glucosamine and chondroitin
- rich in protein
- supports gum and dental health
- increase mobility in dogs with joint pain , hip dysplasia and arthritis

Dogs and cats that suffer with chicken allergies should avoid chicken feet. Try duck feet if available

Importance of Variety

In their natural habitat animals use selective eating habits. They do not eat a well balanced diet on a daily basis but instead hunt for what they are craving and lacking. For instance, if they are lacking iron, zinc or vitamin B they would hunt red meat prey. Domestic dogs are unable to self select and therefore depend on us to feed a well balanced diet over time, depending on their age, health and other individual dogs needs. Therefore, they should be fed at least 4 different proteins per week.

**This does not apply to dogs and cats that are still in the transition phase.

Types of Raw Feeding

PMR - Prey Model Raw (True carnivore believers and cat feeders)

80%meat, sinew, and ligaments, 10% edible bones, 5%liver and 5%other organ meat

PMR feeders do not believe in adding supplements to their dog's or cat's diet and generally do not include any plant, dairy based items or any supplements. This type of raw feeding is based on feeding a whole animal, from head to tail, replicating what an animal would do in the wild. A typical meal for a dog and cat would be, pick up a rabbit, chop it up according to the weight the dog or cat requires to eat and feed. Normally PMR feeders leave fur on the prey as this is known to be a natural dewormer. Many feeders feed rabbit ears as a treat. Most common prey that is fed are whole rabbit, duck and quail.

80% Muscle meat provides essential protein, water-soluble vitamins and amino acids.It is vitally important that muscle meat is made up of protein, heart, gizzards, tongue, lung, trachea and GREEN tripe.

PMR - Prey Model Raw (True carnivore believers and cat feeders)

80%meat, sinew, and ligaments, 10% edible bones, 5%liver and 5%other organ meat

PMR feeders do not believe in adding supplements to their dog's or cat's diet and generally do not include any plant, dairy based items or any supplements. This type of raw feeding is based on feeding a whole animal, from head to tail, replicating what an animal would do in the wild. A typical meal for a dog and cat would be, pick up a rabbit, chop it up according to the weight the dog or cat requires to eat and feed. Normally PMR feeders leave fur on the prey as this is known to be a natural dewormer. Many feeders feed rabbit ears as a treat. Most common prey that is fed are whole rabbit, duck and quail.

80% Muscle meat provides essential protein, water-soluble vitamins and amino acids.It is vitally important that muscle meat is made up of protein, heart, gizzards, tongue, lung, trachea and GREEN tripe.

BARF (Biological Appropriate Raw Food)
Facultative Omnivores Believers
DOGS ONLY

Raw bones, meat and veg

50%meat made up of sinew, ligaments and fat, 20% edible bone, 20% vegetables and fruits, 5%liver and 5% other organs. Included in the diet supplements, healthy oils and vitamins are added.

BARF feeders belief that dogs in the wild eat a significant amount of plant based meals through ingestion of the stomach of their prey. Vegetables should either be fed cooked or liquidised/ mashed to mimic how dogs in the wild would eat them from the stomach of their prey. While mashing them breaks down cellulose it will still retain all nutrients needed.

Most pre-packed meals follow the BARF concept. One of the advantages of feeding pre-packed meals is time. Simply thaw a balanced pre-packed meal and feed. Even though pre-packed meals are well balanced and packed with nutrients, owners should still monitor poop, as every dog is different.

The term SARF is also sometimes used and stands for Species Appropriate Raw Food.

*** There is no definite answer to which type of raw feeding is the best for a dog or the most accurate. Some start with one type and move on to another after some times others feed a mixture of both. The best approach is based on the individual's dog's needs and should be tailor made just for him or her.

Pre made raw

These are ready made raw meals, found in the freezer section bought from the pet store. Never buy ready made pre packed raw dog food from a butcher or local raw supplier as they are not well balanced. They may contain non human grade meat and may contain leftover scraps. **Pre packed raw** should be tested to the highest of standards, nutritionally complete and well balanced and follow the FEDIAF guidelines. If you do prefer buying minced from the butcher make sure the animal is minced including bones in front of you.

Many raw feeders normally start with pre made meals from reputable brands and then move onto to DIY. Others prefer keeping their dog on these pre packed raw brands. They are simple, easy and quick. If you decide to buy pre packed brands, offer some bones like turkey necks or chicken necks to clean their teeth.

It is highly recommended to still check the poop consistency. Each dog and cat is an individual and even though brands follow the guideline of the meat:bone:organ ratio, it may not be the right balance for your pet. If your dog or cat defecates crumbly or with bone fragments than stat mixing the pre made raw with some turkey breast or other boneless meat.

Quantity to Feed

7-10 weeks 10% of total ideal body weight

10-16 weeks 8% of total ideal body weight

16-20 weeks 7% of total ideal body weight

20-24 weeks 6% of total ideal body weight

24-36 weeks 5% of total ideal body weight

36-56 weeks 4% of total ideal body weight

56-68 weeks 3% of total ideal body weight

68 weeks+ 2-3% of total ideal body weight

Adult dogs and cats should be fed 2-3% of their ideal body weight per day. Very active dogs and dogs and cats that need to put on weight need to be fed at least 3% of their body weight. Dogs and cats that need to lose weight or are not active must not be fed more than 2% of their body weight.

Example - Adult Dog/Cat weight 8kgs 8000 x 2.5 = 200 grams per day

As pups and kittens are still growing and developing they require higher amounts of proteins, minerals, and vitamins. Do not be afraid to give them extra food. It is highly recommended that puppies and kittens up to 6 months of age are fed three to four times a day. For instance a 10 week old puppy weighing 4 kgs requires at least 400 grams per day. If fed four times a day, they need to be fed 100 grams per meal.

This is just a guideline and percentages need to be adjusted according to the dog and cat. If dog or cat is losing weight increase quantity. Intact dogs and cats normally eat more whilst spayed or neutered pets need to eat less.

Ideal weight of a dog or cat

Many people have the misconception that dogs and cats need to look bulky and big to be healthy. This is completely wrong on many levels. Obese or even slightly overweight pets come with a lot of mental and health issues. They are more prone to many kinds of cancers, diabetes, heart disease, hypertension, osteoarthritis and degeneration of joints. The ideal weight of a dog or cat is when ribs are not visible but felt. The dog or cat must be well proportioned, waist is easily noticed when viewed from above and a slight abdominal tuck.

Weaning puppies and kittens on a fresh healthy diet gives them a healthy start to life whilst ensuring a long, healthy and fit life.

It is best to transition them slowly from their mums milk onto a fresh diet. Start by introducing them to fresh raw goats milk whilst they are still drinking their mums milk. This will help them in adjusting their system to new fresh food. Once they are completely weaned from the mother start by introducing solids mixed in the raw goats milk. Ensure to mince the proteins and start with leaner proteins such as turkey, chicken and rabbit.

Once all proteins have been properly introduced make sure that they are given a variety of meals.

Transitioning Phase

Introducing proteins should be done slowly. This will indicate if the dog or cat has an intolerance to any protein. If you re adding veg for your dog, avoid organs and vegetables for the first few weeks . We have not included chicken in the second calendar. The reason being is that many dogs and cats are allergic to the food chickens are fed and end up developing allergies. You may either start with chicken or introduce chicken at a later phase when the dog or cat has transitioned. Normally dogs and cats with intolerances toward chicken develop ear infections, marks on skin, severe scratching and severe paw licking.

Sample Calendar 1

*If **home** cooking **all** meat **MUST** be **boneless**, and bone meal powder must be added*

Week 1 Chicken

Week 2 Turkey

Week 3 Rabbit

Week 4 Turkey + Tripe (*For cats start adding chicken hearts in every meal*)

Week 5 Chicken + one or two meal beef

Week 6 Rabbit mixed with fish (80% rabbit 20%fish)

Week 7 Rabbit + Turkey + Chicken + one or two meals venison or duck

Week 8 If no intolerance or allergies appear start giving at least 4 different proteins per week. Introduce eggs very slowly by giving half an egg at the beginning. For dogs start adding veg and organs slowly.

Ideal for DIY

*Remember if home cooking all meat **MUST** be bone less*

- Week 1 - Rabbit (All parts of rabbit, except organs, may be fed including fur, ears, head and tail. Fur is known to be a natural dewormer. Dehydrated ears with fur can be given as a treat)
- Week 2 - Quail and Rabbit. You may give quail in the morning and rabbit in the evening. These are both very lean meats. Avoid any organs and vegetables for now.
- Week 3 - Rabbit Quail and Green Tripe. If you notice any intolerance take a step back or start from the beginning and extend introducing a new protein longer.
- Week 4 - Rabbit Quail Turkey Neck and Green Tripe. Tripe should never be bought from the butcher as they bleach it and remove all enzymes and probiotics. Always buy from the pet shop frozen and ensure there is written GREEN tripe. Feed tripe a maximum of three meals in a week or a tablespoon in every meal all week.
- Week 5 - Turkey, Rabbit and Duck. Introduce a red meat such as duck. Only feed red meat twice or a **maximum** of three meals a week. Red meat is too rich and fatty for the majority of dogs and cats and can easily cause pancreatitis if fed too much.
- Week 6 - Rabbit, Turkey and Quail. Try introducing organs. Remember do not exceed 5 % organs and 5% liver. If you have not introduced muscle meat such as heart and tongue, try introducing it very slowly.

You may also swap duck for minced venison. Some countries may also have certain exotic meats available such as kangaroo, pheasant and goat. Remember do not feed a lot of red meat and do not exceed two to three meals per week. At week 7 start giving an egg twice a week. Start very slowly by giving half an egg the first few times. You may also introduce sprats, sardines and green lipped mussels. The key is moderation and variety.

Some raw feeders alternate proteins by only giving one protein per meal. Others like to give a variety in one meal. There is no set rule. Just as long as at least four proteins are fed (after transition is complete) per **week** then it does not matter. Example of a raw fed meal where a variety of proteins are fed in one meal

1 Sprat,
1 green lipped mussel
Piece of rabbit, quail + organs
Tbsp Tripe,
Tsp kefir
Tbsp Bone broth,
Tsp Grinded pumpkin seeds
1/4 Tsp Spirulina
Tsp raw apple cider vinegar
Cranberry probiotic.

Recommended Fish to Feed

Oily fish are a great source of omega 3
- anchovies
- carp
- herring (bloater, kipper and hilsa are types of herring)
- jack (also known as scad, horse mackerel and trevally)
- mackerel
- pilchards
- salmon
- sardines
- sprats
- trout
- tuna (fresh)**
- whitebait

**Canned Tuna is not considered an oily fish as once it is canned it the amount of long chain omega 3 is highly reduced.

Fish is a great source of protein and contains a lot of Omega-3 fatty acids and therefore are rich with antioxidants and anti- inflammatory properties that help dogs and cats with joint and mobility issues. Fish is low in saturated fats. It also helps in giving a shine to your pet's coat.

Small oily fish such as sardines in water, smelt and mackerel are ideal to feed. During the transitioning phase fish should always be introduced as one of the last proteins. Later on in the course we will discuss further how to best transition your pet.

Amounts to feed per week-
Small dogs and cats - 30g of small oily fish per 4.5 kgs of body weight.
Medium to large dogs - 90g of small oily fish per 13.6 kgs of body weight
Therefore if your dog weighs 8 kgs do not feed more than 55gr of fish per week.

Fish and organs must be frozen for at least three weeks before feeding to kill any parasites.

If you pet does not like fish you may supplement them with fish oil such as krill oil or salmon oil.

Recipes For Raw Feeding Feeding

Below are some sample recipes. Weight and quantity varies depending on the dog or cat. Adjust accordingly. If using one of the recipes for cats ensure to add beef or chicken hearts for extra taurine and omit any veggie ingredients.

Recipe 1

Ingredients

- Half quail including quail Organs
- One sprat
- Half teaspoon psyllium husk
- One egg
- Piece of rabbit
- Tsp grinded pumpkin seeds
- Tsp of bone broth

Recipe 2

Ingredients

- One green lipped mussel
- Part quail including organs
- ⅓ duck neck ,
- Part rabbit
- Few drops of kefir
- Ground pumpkin seed
- Pork and Veal cubes
- Teaspoon of pork brain
- Cooked or liquidised veggie mix
- One egg

DIY Minced

The recipes over leaf are great to use to stuff kongs and trachea, or simply in their bowl. Kongs and tracheas are great for mental stimulation. The below recipes can also be used to feed cats.

Ingredients - Total grams - 3,400

Boneless meat : all minced
600 grams turkey breast
600 grams chicken breast
200 grams gizzards
300 grams venison

Meat with bones : all minced
800 grams quail
600 grams chicken drumsticks
200 grams chicken wings

100 grams chicken liver

It is recommended to remove all skin. There is enough fat in todays meat.

Mix all ingredients together and stuff the kong with the mixture.

Ingredients

Boneless meat : all minced
600 grams turkey breast
600 grams chicken breast
1 whole quail

Meat with bones : all minced
2 whole quails incl organs
1 whole rabbit incl organs

Supplements

Supplements are something that we must be careful with as they are not as well-regulated as food is. Almost anything can be sold under the name 'supplement' even if it has no nutritional value. It is a good idea to discuss anything you are thinking of supplementing in your dog's diet with a holistic vet first, and to research thoroughly. Some supplements have great ingredients on paper, but the form is not readily available to the body - so you may end up producing very high-quality urine at no benefit to the dog!

Most dogs that are on a complete well balanced diet have no need for supplements. However, a dog's metabolism and needs can change, and their nutritional requirements will change with it. If you give your dog a good quality food but they are not looking first rate or acting as they should for their age, then additional nutrients may be required. The first thing to do is get a full health check with a holistic vet to obtain their opinion on general condition. They can do a physical examination, carry out blood and urine tests and highlight any obvious problems. The vet may then recommend a specific supplement for early intervention.

Only give a supplement if your pet needs it, not just because it's the latest product on the market or your friend gives it to their pet. Only give supplements where you know exactly what is in them, by reading the list of ingredients. If you give a supplement to your dog and there is no response after six to eight weeks, then stop giving it. Likewise, if they have a negative response stop feeding it. We always recommend to buy supplements from an organic health shop.

So when should we add supplements?

Supplements help in recovering from an illness, trauma, injury and promotes healing.

Dogs that have allergies or have cancer do not produce enough vitamin C and E and tend to drain out when stressed. and therefore supplements that contain vitamin C and E are highly recommended to help with healing.

Dogs that suffer with joint problems such as hip dysplasia and arthritis need nutraceuticals. These nutriments are found in trachea of a cattle and green or blue lipped mussels. You can either feed them fresh or buy supplements in powder form. These aid in preventing the issue escalating further and reduce symptoms such as pain.

Glucosamine, Chondroitin and Curcumin are also supplements that are recommend to help with joint issues. When feeding a dog or cat raw that has joint problems ensure to increase joints in their diet. Chicken are a great source of glucosamine and chondroitin and are soft enough to feed senior dogs and other dogs with dental issues.

Always ensure to find a brand and product that works well for your dog. Each dog is different and what works on one dog may not be good for another. *Most home cooking recipes need at least one supplement.*

Poop Consistency

Poop should always be firm, leaving no skid marks on the floor. If poop is too crumbly or the dog is straining to defecate then you are feeding too much bone. Decrease bone content and add boneless meat such as boneless quail or boneless rabbit. If you are feeding pre-made meals that have a high bone quantity and the dog is struggling to defecate then add boneless meat from the butcher.

If poop is soft then you need to add bone content. Add a chicken or duck neck. If poop is black in colour and very soft then you are feeding too many organs. Liver should never exceed 5% and organs should never exceed 10% as too much vitamin A becomes toxic.

Basic DIY
 ratio 80:10:10 - Meat :Bone:Liver+Organs

If you are finding bone fragments or your dog or cat is yelping when eliminating then the bone content needs to be decreased. This may also happen if you are feeding a particular bone that your dog's stomach does not digest properly. This normally happens with ribs and lamb bones. This type of bones have too little meat and should be avoided unless they are minced.

Bones need an acidic stomach to digest well. Kibble fed dogs and cats do not produce enough acid and the stomach may become "lazy". On very rare occasions a previously kibble fed dog or cat's stomach will not be able to digest bone properly. This may also be due to an underlying medical condition. If you notice that this is happening and your pet is eliminating the bone whole do not feed whole bones instead always mince bones or feed pre made ready raw only. In this case consult your holistic vet to make a through check up

Frequently Asked Questions

- **Should I freeze meat for a particular number of days?**
We normally recommend buying human grade meat. That means meat bought from a licensed butcher. This type of meat does not need to be frozen as it is tested for any type of worms before it is placed on the market. However all types of seafood and organs need to be frozen for at least three weeks.

- **Do I need to deworm my dog?**
Dogs pick up worms from sniffing contaminated floors, soil, poop or other dogs' backside. If human grade meat or authorised pre made meals are bought, and seafood and organs are frozen for three weeks there is no need to deworm your dog unless there is a need to. We recommend grinding some pumpkin seeds as this is known to be a natural dewormer.

- **Is it too early to transition a puppy / kitten that I just brought home or too late to transition a senior dog or cat?**
Breeders that raw feed their dogs and cats wean their puppies and kittens with raw at five weeks, therefore it is never too early to transition. It is actually better to transition them to raw once they are still young as they will adjust to the transition more easily. It is also never too late to transition a senior dog. If you feed a well balanced diet tailored to his or her needs then the benefits of raw will definitely have a good impact on his or her health and well being.

- **I have young children, should I worry that they could get salmonella?**

When handling meat, whether it is for us to eat or for our pets, proper hygiene must always take a priority. Wash your hands and surfaces after handling meat. Train your pet to eat on a towel or train the dog pr cat to eat in his or her crate and place a towel at the bottom. Also wash your hands after picking up their feaces. Common sense should tell you not to eat their feaces.

- **Can my pet get salmonella?**

Dog's and cats's saliva is naturally equipped with antibacterial properties called lysozyme. This type of enzyme destroys any harmful bacteria. Their short gut is equipped to move food quickly and therefore does not give bacteria time to colonise. The low PH in the stomach also helps the bacteria to move along. The majority of cases where dogs or cats had salmonella is from kibble fed dogs. There are many dry food brands that have been taken of the shelves due to bacteria and moulds that produce a deadly toxin. The starches, sugars and fats that are found in dry food brands are more prone to bacteria than human grade raw food. We never recommend buying " ready made raw **dog** food" from a butcher as these are leftovers which are not placed on the market. Always buy meat from the butcher that you would eat - sold for human consumption and therefore is human grade therefore tested. We also do not recommend buying from a local raw feeder ready mixed dog food. Many times the mix does not contain human grade meat. Normally the mix contains proteins that are cheap to sell for instance beef, chicken and tripe. Also we need to understand that one size does not fit all dogs. Many dogs develop allergies from chicken. Red meat should **not** be fed on a daily basis as this will cause chronic or acute pancreatitis

- **My dog is vomiting bile or yellow liquid**

Bile or yellow liquid is acid reflux. It normally happens when the dog is hungry. Ensure that you are feeding the right amount. The percentages given are just guidelines ad some dogs may need a higher quantity. Try adjusting the timings of when you feed the dog, and offer an additional small meal during lunch time. Not all dogs are the same. Some would prefer one meal a day only, whilst others need to eat three times a day even as adults.

- **How do I transition my dog or cat?**

There are two methods. First method which is the easiest and fastest way is to stop dry food in the evening and start on raw straight away in the morning. Animals digest dry food and raw differently and therefore starting raw food straight away on an empty stomach is recommended. This will avoid their stomach getting upset. Second method is by transitioning slowly by adding raw and decreasing dry food over time. For instance, for the first four days in the bowl you would put 75% raw and 25% dry food. For the second four days, 50% raw and 50% dry food. This method is preferred for dogs that may be fussy and picky eaters. Cats become addicted to dry food due to the high sugar content, therefore the second method is much easier. 75%wet food 25% raw for the first few days and so on. With kittens it is normally much easier and a fast transition method is usually used.

- **My dog or cat will not eat pre-made meals, however he prefers chunks from the butcher or vice versa.**

Some animals like their raw meat as they would eat it in the wild and therefore they will only eat raw meat bones like turkey necks, rabbit legs, quail etc. Whilst other dogs may be too laid back and prefer eating pre-made ready raw brands. Others may prefer one brand of pre-made over the other. This is absolutely normal. You have two options. Either give your dog his or her preferred meal type or if you are up to some tough love try the following method. Put the food down for twenty minutes, if he or she does not eat it, place it back in the fridge and try again in the evening. Dogs can go without food for four days. Once they are hungry they will eat what is offered to them.

With cats you must never use the tough love method as cats cannot be starved.

We just transitioned our pet and he is vomiting up all the raw.

Pre-made meals are ready mixed with vegetables and organs. Some dogs that may have an immune compromised system may take a while for their stomach to settle. This is perfectly normal. Some dogs may need a bland meal to start with. Have a look at the sample calendar in the previous pages and start preparing the meals yourself. You may also try adding some probiotics and enzymes to the meal. We do recommend to start offering meals three or four times a day for the first few weeks, even for adult dogs and cats. This will help with the transition and digesting the food much easier. Dogs and cats with liver issues or who suffer with pancreatitis must be fed small portions more frequently - three or four times a day.

My pet suffers from pancreatitis. Can he eat raw?
The great thing about raw is that you can adjust the meals according to your dog's medical needs. The reason most dogs suffer from pancreatitis is because of a high fat diet or due to too much red meat. Some dogs may even get pancreatitis after surgery or trauma.

Generally speaking dogs recovering or have a history of pancreatitis must stay on lean white meats only. Always remove any skin or fat. No potatoes, grains, rice or carb of any kind. If you are going to try introducing some red meat do not feed lamb or beef they are very high in fat. Start with a small amount of lean venison meat. Watch out for their poop texture. Some dogs that suffer with an inflamed pancreas do not tolerate any organs. In this case it is better to avoid both red meat, fish and organs. Broccoli and spinach are great fillers. No oily fish, however if the dog can tolerate some fish feed white non oily fish only.

Summary

- Always seek a veterinarian that supports raw, ideally a holistic one.
- Every dog is different, feed according to your dogs needs
- Always introduce proteins one by one. Once all introduced ensure that they get a good variety of different meats, bones and organs
- Constipated, crumply poop - add more meat and less bone
  Soft poop - less meat and more bone
- Never give more then two or three meals a week with red meat in it
- Always freeze fish and organs for at least 2 or 3 weeks
- History with pancreatitis feed only white meat and bones, little organ as low as 1%
- Always buy human grade meat and ensure that pre made raws also provide human grade meat
- Only give supplements to your dog after speaking to your holistic vet. They will guide you on recommending which supplements the dog needs according to their health and needs. Feeding the appropriate food needed is better then giving supplements.
- Finally MODERATION AND BALANCE IS KEY. Always seek a veterinarian that supports raw, ideally a holistic one.

Charts

Raw MuscleMeat 80%		Offal 10%	Bones 10%	Veggies/ Fruits (Optional)	Supplements (Optional)
Poultry / Lamb / Goat		5% Liver	Poultry Carcass	Berries	Spirulina
			Poultry feet	Beets & Carrots	Tumeric
			Poultry wings	Spinach	Raw honey
Beef / Rabbit		*Other 5 %*	Poultry Necks	Kale	Kefir
			Poultry head	Pumpkin	Plain Greek Yogurt
		Spleen	Rabbit head	Apples	Ground egg shells
Game / Pork		Testicles Kidney Pancreas Brain	Rabbit legs	Cranberries	Fish oil
			Whole quail	Shitake Mushrooms	Krill oil
Fish		1 egg twice or three times per week		Courgettes	Coconut oil
				Banana	Chia Seeds
				Pineapple	Ground Pumpkin Seeds
Also Muscle Meat • Hearts • Trachea • Lungs • Gizzards • Tongue • Diaphram • Green tripe *Should not exceed 25%-40%* *except cats*		**Poo** White - too much bone Soft - too little bone Black - too much offal Yellow - intolerance		Cucumbers	
				Watermelon	
				Broccoli	
		How much to feed Adults 2-3% of body weight Adjust according to energy levels			

The following is a guideline of how much % bone each animal contains. This is just a guideline and varies, depending on the size of animal when bought.

Turkey -
Whole Turkey 22%
Turkey Neck   48%
Turkey Wing   36%
Turkey Back   52%
Turkey Thigh 22%
Turkey Leg   40%

Chicken -
Whole Chicken 30%
Chicken Head 72%
Chicken Neck 34%
Chicken Wing 44%
Chicken Rib Cages 80%
Chicken Back 42%
Chicken Foot 60%
Chicken Leg Quarter 32%
Chicken Leg 28%
Chicken Thigh 22%

Duck
Whole Duck 29%
Duck Head 76%
Duck Frame 81%
Duck Neck 51%
Duck Wing 40%
Duck Foot 61%

Rabbit
Whole Rabbit 28%
Rabbit Head   75%
Rabbit front leg 15%
Rabbit hind leg 14%
Rabbit spine/back 15%
Rabbit front quarter 23%
Rabbit hindquarter 17%

The following game can also be fed -
Whole Quail - 10%
Guinea hen - 17%
Squab (pigeon) - 23%
Pheasant whole 14%
Cornish Game Hen - 39%
Whole goose -19%
Dove whole - 23%

Reminder - These are just guidelines and factors such as age, medical history and breed should always be considered.

Senior Dogs

As animals get older they require more medical attention. Even the most well kept pets, develop joint problems. Fresh feeding helps to prevent and prolong certain medical issues from occurring, however sometimes it is inevitable.

Over weight pets puts pressure on their joints and therefore it is of up most importance that we know what the ideal weight for our dogs and cats is.

As our pets age it is recommended to speak to our holistic vet to recommend some supplements suitable for them.

As they get older their physical activity slows down and therefore so does their metabolism. Their calorie intake should be reduced. Adding supplements, digestive enzymes and vitamins can benefit them greatly. Senior pets need a higher protein ratio. If you notice that they are struggling to defecate add more meat and less bones or bone powder. You may opt to give one boneless meal a day.

Senior pets that struggle to defecate can benefit also from adding more fibre in their meals. It is quite normal for them to have bouts of diarrhoea or in the case with dogs wind. This is because they may not be able to digest their food as well as they used to.

Benefits of Ingredients and Supplements

Garlic There is a whole debate on wether or not garlic is toxic or not to dogs. For garlic to be toxic your pet needs to ingest 15 to 30 grams per one kg of dogs body weight. This means a 40 kgs dog needs to eat 150 cloves of garlic for it to be toxic.

Garlic detoxifies a dogs body and helps to eliminate any harmful bacteria. It prevents any blood cloths from forming, helps to prevent formation of tumours works as an antibiotic and is a great way to eliminate fleas and ticks naturally. It is known to help fight certain cancers such as colon, lung, stomach and rectum. *Please note that your dog needs to be healthy before adding garlic to their diet and my interact with certain medications. Not recommended for cats*

Parsley is a natural source of Vitamin C which helps with immune support. It contains vitamin A which also helps with immune support and with your furry friend's vision. Parsley is also know to help fight infections like UTI however if your pet suffers with and type of kidney *disease it is best to avoid parsley.*

Organic Eggs

- High in protein, amino and fatty acids, vitamins, folate, iron, selenium and riboflavin.
- Improves texture of skin and coat
- Stronger teeth and bones

Dosage: Always start gradually and increase to two or three eggs over a week.

Green or blue lipped mussels

- It is a natural inflammatory
- It reduces joint pain and protects the cartilage
- It boosts your pet's immunity
- It strengthens the bones
- It prevents the development of arthritis in your four-legged friend

If you do not wish to feed raw you can either cook or add green lipped mussel powder

Cranberries are known to help with preventing and treating urinary tract infections. They are a great source of fibre and contain vitamins A, B1, B2 and C. They are **high** in antioxidants and aid with lowering cholesterol levels.

Pureed & Cooked Leafy Greens

- Kale is high in vitamin K, A and iron. This aids in strengthening bone health, vision and boosts the immune system.
- Spinach contains potassium, magnesium and vitamins B6, B9 and E
- Broccoli is high in Vitamin K, potassium and calcium. Vitamin K is essential for strong bones and higher bone density and is essential ingredient for growing puppies

Fish oils

- provide essential fatty acids which offer natural inflammation regulation.
- Helpful whilst undergoing treatment of cancer, allergies, kidney disease, heart disease and diabetes.

Flax seed oil

- Benefits are
- High in alpha linolenic omega-3
- Helps with inflammatory diseases
- Reduces constipation
- Gives the coat and skin a silky shine
- Great for pets with mobility issues
- Substitute for pets with fish and fish oil allergies
- Boosts the immune system and therefore helps fights off mild allergies

Dosage 1 tsp for small dogs, 2 tsp for medium dogs, and 1 tsp for large dogs per day.

Coconut oil

- Coconut oil is known to help pets lose weight whilst giving them more energy.
- It improves dogs bad breath and pet odour
- Gives their coat a lovely shine
- Improved digestion by increasing nutrient absorption and helps with ibs and colitis
- Relieves itchy skin and improves eczema
- Helps with bites and stings
- Prevents and treats yeast and fungal infection
- Promotes wound healing when topically applied
- Helps soothe hot spots
- Aids with coughing
- Prevents sicknesses and diseases

Dosage : An optimal dose of 1 tsp for every 10 pounds of weight Always start slowly if no adverse reaction are seen increase to recommended dose gradually

Pumpkin Seeds

Must always be served grinded

- High in fiber therefore Improves digestion
- Helps dislodge kidney stones
- Natural dewormer and fights of parasites
- High in magnesium
- Reduces risk of heart disease
- Regulates blood sugar and pressure
- Antioxidants and fatty acids help promote dogs urinary health
- Helps with inflammation especially arthritis and hip elbow dysplasia

Contains -

- Potassium for muscle support
- Zinc for immune function, hormone regulation, and brain activity
- Iron, phosphorus, and magnesium for red blood cell function
- Calcium for strong, healthy bone and teeth growth, as well as fighting cancers

Enzymes Digestive enzymes are proteins which help in breaking down complex nutrients which in turn can be absorbed by the small intestine. Cooking above 48 Celsius destroys enzymes that is found in food and therefore your dog or cat's body needs to produce these enzymes to digest the food. If these enzymes are not present then your dog or cat will have enzyme deficiency even though you are preparing a well balanced diet. Enzymes supplements are recommended for elderly pets, pets that are either ill or recovering from an illness, pets that need to gain weight and those that have been fed an inappropriate diet for a long time. Green tripe is packed with enzymes.

Pre and Probiotics

Probiotics are present in the gastrointestinal tract. This live bacteria aids in creating a hospitable environment for digestion. Prebiotics feeds this live bacteria and together they eliminate any harmful bacteria.

They are highly recommended to be given after a course of antibiotics. As probiotics is a live bacteria it is highly recommended to be bought and fed fresh. Examples of probiotics is fresh raw goats milk and fresh kefir.

Spirulina

- This tiny alga is packed with nutrients. A single tablespoon (7 grams) of dried spirulina powder contains :
- Protein 60% : 4 grams
- Vitamin B1 (thiamine)
- Vitamin B2 (riboflavin)
- Vitamin B3 (niacin)
- Copper: 21%
- Iron: 11%
- It also contains decent amounts of magnesium, potassium and manganese .
- Spirulina is a fantastic source of antioxidants like vitamins E and C
- Contains powerful anti-inflammatory properties particularly GLA
- Beneficial to pets with allergic skin conditions, cancer and heart disease.

  Do not give spirulina to dogs with history of liver disease

Slippery elm powder

Slippery elm is a safe non toxic herb which is found in the inner bark of a treat. If your pet is on any medication slippery elm should be give 1 to 2 hrs apart. When to use slippery elm:

- Reduces inflammation within the body
- Aids with healing diarrhoea, colitis, gastroenteritis and IBS
- Helps pets that suffer with pancreatitis
- Aids in respiratory issues like colds, sore throat, coughs collapsed trachea, bronchitis and acid reflux
- Heals minor wounds, burns, ulcers and hotspots

Dosage : quarter of a teaspoon for every 10 pound of dog or cat's body weight

Kelp

- High in fiber
- Aids with allergy symptoms
- Boosts immune system
- Supports glandur system
- Reduces plaque and tartar in teeth
- Helps support tissue repair and healthy circulation
- Promotes healthy skin and coat

Bladderwrack

- This is a form of kelp which is rich in iodine and calcium
- Increases metabolism and boosts the immune system
- Helps in treating over or under active thyroid

active thyroid

Organic Tumeric
- Acts as a natural pain relief especially for Arthritis joint pain
- Helps with pets suffering with heart disease
- Prevents and treats pets with cancer
- Known to reduce size of tumours
- Boosts the immune system which helps to fight of allergies
- Natural warming herb with helps pets feel less cold in winter
- Prevents toxins in building in the liver and pancreas
- Promotes healing pets with liver and pancreas issues

Dosage 1/4 teaspoon for every 10 pounds of body weight

As turmeric is a natural blood thinner is not recommended on pets that are on any blood thinning medication. Always consult your holistic vet before you start adding any supplements. A rare side effect is constipation. If this happens to your pet reduce the daily recommended dose. Always introduce turmeric slowly and never exceed the recommended dosage.

Milk Thistle

- Reduces inflammation in kidney and liver issues
- Aids in secondary autoimmune issues like tumors or skin problems that would have resulted from a liver condition
- May also help with Cushing's disease, diabetes and Pancreatitis

- **Psyllium Husk**
- Helps dogs and cats that suffer with anal glands
- Cleanses and gently removes toxins and waste from the body

Raw Apple Cider Vinegar aids with digestion by balancing the PH in a dogs body, relieves muscle soreness especially for senior dogs, prevents urinary tract infections, fights against yeast infections and relives allergy symptoms.

Please note that these ingredients are a great source of supplements to add to your dogs diet, to maintain and improve your dogs overall health. They should in no way substitute any conventional medicine that your vet may have prescribed. We always recommend speaking to a holistic vet that supports **both** herbal and conventional medicine.

THE END

*A **big thank you goes** to my inspirations and the loves of my life Ollie, Benji & Betty, our furry cat cousins Phantom & Pupa and our kitty friends Harry and William.*

Lightning Source UK Ltd.
Milton Keynes UK
UKHW021052050221
378299UK00007B/98

9 781034 299516